STAR PATTERNS IN THE SKY

by Dixie Marshall
illustrated by Robert Roper

Harcourt
SCHOOL PUBLISHERS

Printed in China

ISBN 10: 0-15-350696-2
ISBN 13: 978-0-15-350696-3

Ordering Options
ISBN 10: 0-15-350600-8 (Grade 3 On-Level Collection)
ISBN 13: 978-0-15-350600-0 (Grade 3 On-Level Collection)
ISBN 10: 0-15-357913-7 (package of 5)
ISBN 13: 978-0-15-357913-4 (package of 5)

2 3 4 5 6 7 8 9 10 985 12 11 10 09 08 07

People have always enjoyed watching the stars in the night sky. On a clear night, you might see thousands of stars. A star is really a huge ball of burning gases. It is the burning gases that cause the stars to light up in the sky. The sun is also a star. Its light reflects off the surface of the earth. It is the closest star to our planet.

Early in the evening, faraway stars appear over the horizon. As the night goes on, the stars seem to move across the sky from east to west. It is not the stars that move, but the earth. The stars have a fixed position in space. That is, they do not move like the earth or the moon. Earth rotates, or spins on its axis. As the earth turns, the pattern of stars marches across the sky.

Stars that are over the center of Earth look like they move in a straight line across the sky. At the North and South Poles, stars look like they move in a circle. This is also due to the spinning of the earth. These same stars can be seen from the poles all year round.

People on the top half of the earth see different stars than people who live on the bottom half. A person who lives in the United States sees different stars than a person who lives in South America or Australia.

Early people such as the Greeks watched the stars. They did not know that the stars were fixed in space. The Greeks made up stories to explain why the stars moved.

The Greeks also saw imaginary pictures or patterns in groups of stars. They identified the pictures as familiar people or animals. Today we call these star pictures *constellations*. If you have ever seen the Big Dipper overhead, you were looking at a constellation.

The Big Dipper is part of a larger group of stars called *Ursa Major*. That means "Great Bear" in Latin. If you connect the stars of *Ursa Major*, you can see the head and huge paws of a bear. The handle of the Big Dipper forms the tail of the bear.

Native Americans told stories about the star patterns in the sky, too. Some Native Americans thought the bowl of the Big Dipper was the body of a bear. The three stars that make up the handle were people chasing the bear.

Each night, the Big Dipper constellation appears to move in a circle overhead. In the spring and summer, the Big Dipper is high overhead. During the winter, the Big Dipper is closer to the horizon.

You can find the North Star by looking at the Big Dipper. The two stars at the end of the Big Dipper point to the North Star. The North Star is the last star at the tip of the handle of the Little Dipper.

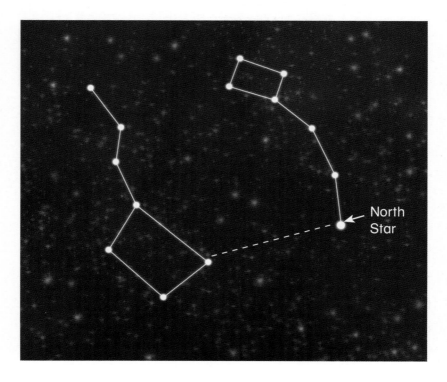

North Star

In all, there are eighty-eight named constellations in
the sky. The star patterns form many different animals.
There are a dragon, a swan, a crab, and a bull, to name
a few. Star patterns form pictures of people, too. There
are a water carrier, a hunter, and an archer whose
steady arm holds a bow and arrow.

Some star groups can only be seen during certain seasons. At other times, they dip below the horizon.

One constellation you can see best in the winter is Orion, the hunter. Three stars line up in a row to form the hunter's belt. Two stars form above his knees. Two other stars make up the shoulders. The lion that Orion is holding is made up of five stars.

At the end of winter, you can begin to see the star pattern Cancer, the crab. This constellation has four stars that make up its body and two stars that form the claws.

Another star pattern you see in the spring is Leo, the lion. This star pattern has the shape of a lion's head and mane as well as its body.

In summertime, some different star patterns can be seen. One constellation is of Hercules, who was a great Greek soldier. Some star patterns are of animals that Hercules fought. In fact, Cancer the Crab and Leo the Lion were two of these animals.

Hercules can be seen kneeling in the sky. Four stars form his body in the shape of a square. As summer passes, Hercules is high overhead. Then, in October, he disappears below the horizon.

Another well-known star pattern is that of the winged horse, Pegasus. In the sky, you can see the front part of the horse with a neck and two legs. Stars create the body of the horse in a shape that looks like a square. In the United States, you can see Pegasus from August through fall. If you live in South America, there is evidence of Pegasus overhead during the end of winter and spring.

As fall turns into winter, you can once again see the constellation Orion. The pattern of stars repeats itself each year. Each night a pattern of people and animals marches across the sky. To the early people, the stars were a source of myths and stories. Now, we know more about the stars. When you look up at the night sky, what animals and people do you see?

Think Critically

1. Why do the stars appear to move across the sky each night?

2. Which of the constellations you read about would you be able to see each spring?

3. Why do you think early people made up stories about the stars?

4. Why do different stars appear during different seasons?

5. What did you learn about constellations that surprised you? Explain.

 Science

High Up in the Sky Find some examples of constellations in a book. Then draw some constellations on a piece of paper. Can you see the pictures in the stars that the ancient Greeks saw?

School-Home Connection With a family member, look for constellations in the sky. You can also make up your own constellations if you use your imagination!

Word Count: 905